TOP 10 BASKETBALL SCORING SMALL FORWARDS

Nathan Aaseng

SPORTS TOP 10

Enslow Publishers, Inc.

40 Industrial Road   PO Box 38
Box 398   Aldershot
Berkeley Heights, NJ 07922   Hants GU12 6BP
USA   UK

http://www.enslow.com

Library of Congress Cataloging-in-Publication Data

Aaseng, Nathan.
      Top 10 basketball scoring small forwards / Nathan Aaseng.
         p. cm. — (Sports top 10)
      Includes bibliographical references and index.
      Summary: Discusses the basketball careers of ten of the best small
forwards in the game: Paul Arizin, Rick Barry, Elgin Baylor, Larry Bird, Alex
English, Julius Erving, John Havlicek, Grant Hill, Scottie Pippen, and Glen Rice.
      ISBN 0-7660-1152-6
      1. Forwards (Basketball)—United States—Biography—Juvenile literature.
2. Forwards (Basketball)—Rating of—United States—Juvenile literature.
[1. Basketball players.] I. Title. II. Title: Top ten basketball scoring small
forwards. III. Series.
GV884.A1A25 1999
796.323'092'273—dc21
    [B]   98-44953
                                              CIP
                                              AC

Printed in the United States of America

10 9 8 7 6 5 4 3 2 1

To Our Readers:
All Internet addresses in this book were active and appropriate when we
went to press. Any comments or suggestions can be sent by e-mail to
Comments@enslow.com or to the address on the back cover.

Illustration Credits: Andrew D. Bernstein/NBA Photos, pp. 18, 21, 22; Dick
Raphael/NBA Photos, p. 10; Jim Cummins/NBA Photos, p. 29; Naismith
Memorial Basketball Hall of Fame, pp. 7, 9, 14, 17, 26, 30, 33; Norm Perdue,
1995, p. 42; Norm Perdue, 1996, pp. 38, 41, 45; Norm Perdue, 1997, pp. 35,
37; Rick Barry/NBA Photos, p. 13; Scott Cunningham/NBA Photos, p. 25.

Cover Illustration: Norm Perdue, 1997.

Cover Description: Grant Hill of the Detroit Pistons.

Interior Design: Richard Stalzer.

CONTENTS

INTRODUCTION

ATTENTION, LADIES AND GENTLEMEN! They soar through the air with the greatest of ease.[1] They defy gravity as they twist around obstacles in midair. They fire a ball through a small hoop from twenty-three feet away without touching the rim. They are pro basketball's small forwards: some of the most graceful and spectacular athletes in the world today.

Only in pro basketball, the land of the giants, would these players be labeled *small* anything. The shortest of them stands about six-feet four-inches tall. The tallest, at six-feet nine-inches, towers over average humans.

The term *small forward* is relatively new. Until the late 1960s, coaches put shorter, quicker players at guard. Centers were the largest players on the court. Forwards were in-between players. They were tall and strong. They could score and defend close to the basket and from medium range.

But then, coaches found that a quick, athletic forward could drive his larger and less mobile opponents dizzy. This would make him tough to guard. Teams began to rely on one of these small forwards, along with a power forward who could provide size and muscle under the basket.

There have been so many outstanding small forwards since the position was created that some great players had to left be out of this book. Dominique Wilkins, the flashy "Human Highlight Film" of the Atlanta Hawks, and the superquick James Worthy of the great Lakers teams of the 1980s are just two examples. Charles Barkley holds his own with the players in this book, but is not in the book because he played more as a power forward than as a small forward in his peak years.

Each of the game's great small forwards has brought his own special style to the position. John Havlicek was a nonstop cyclone who wore down his opponents. Elgin Baylor

combined muscle with acrobatic offensive drives. Julius
Erving revolutionized the game with his gravity-defying
dunks. Larry Bird was not a leaper but excelled at passing
and shooting. Scottie Pippen terrorized opponents with his
defensive play. Alex English quietly led his team in scoring
virtually every game. On the court, Grant Hill could do
everything well. Rick Barry, Glen Rice, and Paul Arizin
were sharpshooters who could light up the scoreboard like
pinball machines.

All of these players have been regular members of pro
basketball All-Pro teams and All-Star Games. Their colorful
wizardry with the basketball has helped make their sport
popular throughout the world.

CAREER STATISTICS

Player	Years	Games	FG%	Rebounds	Assists	Steals	Blocks	Points	Average
PAUL ARIZIN	1950–52 1954–62	713	.421	6,129	1,665	*	*	16,266	22.8
RICK BARRY**	1965–67 1972–80	794	.449	5,168	4,017	1,104*	269*	18,395	23.2
ELGIN BAYLOR	1958–72	846	.431	11,463	3,650	*	*	23,149	27.4
LARRY BIRD	1979–92	897	.496	8,974	5,695	1,556	755	21,791	24.3
ALEX ENGLISH	1976–91	1,193	.507	6,538	4,351	1,067	833	25,613	21.5
JULIUS ERVING**	1976–87	836	.507	5,601	3,224	1,508	1,293	18,364	22.0
JOHN HAVLICEK	1962–78	1,270	.439	8,007	6,114	476*	117*	26,395	20.8
GRANT HILL	1994–	311	.471	2,572	2,035	511	211	6,434	20.7
SCOTTIE PIPPEN	1987–	833	.483	5,658	4,444	1,771	765	14,987	18.0
GLEN RICE	1989–	718	.463	3,412	1,641	812	226	14,899	20.8

*Statistics for steals and blocks are not complete for all players because the NBA did not keep
them as an official statistic until the 1973–74 season.
**Does not include statistics from the American Basketball Association (ABA).

PAUL ARIZIN

TODAY, PRO SCOUTS FOLLOW the top prospects even before they hit high school. They would never even look at a kid like Paul Arizin. Arizin loved sports but was cursed with an awkward body. He got flattened by larger players in football. He was very nearsighted, so he had to struggle to hit a baseball. As for boxing, "A couple of bloody noses convinced me I'd never make it as a boxing champion."[1]

In desperation, he turned to basketball. But he never made the team at LaSalle High School in Philadelphia. When he moved on to Villanova University, he kept playing for fun in recreational leagues. While doing so, he developed a smooth, one-handed jump shot. He also grew to six-feet four-inches. When the school's coach heard about this kid scoring more than 30 points a game in the recreational league, he asked Arizin to try out for the team.

Arizin made the team but sat on the bench for seven games. When the coach finally put him into a game, Arizin went scoreless. But in the ninth game of the season, he flipped in 10 points. From there, Arizin's career was like a runaway train. The following year, he scored 85 points in a single game! He wound up with 1,596 points in his three seasons. The Philadelphia Warriors selected the hometown boy with the first choice in the 1950 NBA draft.

The jump shot was "Pitchin' Paul's" trademark. By waiting until he was at the highest point of his jump before releasing the ball, he made his shots difficult to block. One of the game's top coaches, Joe Lapchick, described Arizin's jump shot as "perfection."[2] The high-jumping Arizin also surprised his new coaches by leading his team

PAUL ARIZIN

Paul Arizin was known for his smooth shooting touch.
Arizin led the NBA in scoring for the 1951–52 season.

in rebounding. This, combined with his 17.2 scoring average, helped vault the Warriors from near the bottom of the standings to first place in his rookie season.

In 1951–52, Arizin averaged 25.4 points per game, to end George Mikan's three-year reign as the NBA's top scorer. Proving his toughness, he set an NBA record by playing 63 minutes of an overtime game against the Lakers.

At the peak of his game, Arizin left the league for two years while he was in the U.S. Marines. When he returned to Philadelphia in 1954, the team had a new scoring star, center Neil Johnston. It took time for Arizin to adjust his game to suit Johnston. Despite the fact that Johnston and Arizin finished 1–2 in scoring that season, the Warriors finished last in their division. But in the 1955–56 season, the Warriors won the NBA title. Arizin followed that up with his second scoring title in 1956–57, posting a 25.6 average.

Arizin was still at the top of his game in 1962 when the Warriors moved to San Francisco. This time it was his turn to say "No thanks." After reaching ten thousand points faster than anyone else in NBA history, he retired.

PAUL ARIZIN

BORN: April 9, 1928, Philadelphia, Pennsylvania.

HIGH SCHOOL: LaSalle High School, Philadelphia, Pennsylvania.

COLLEGE: Villanova University.

PRO: Philadelphia Warriors, 1950–1952, 1954–1962.

HONORS: NBA scoring leader, 1952, 1957; NBA field goal percentage leader, 1952; NBA minutes leader, 1952, 1955; NBA All-Star, 1952, 1955–1962; NBA All-Star MVP, 1952; elected to Basketball Hall of Fame, 1977.

During his career, Arizin made the All-NBA first team three times.

Internet Address

http://www.nba.com/history/arizin_bio.html

RICK BARRY

Although surrounded by Bullets defenders, Rick Barry makes room for a shot.

RICK BARRY

A TALL, GANGLY MAN WALKS to the free-throw line late in a championship game. He holds the ball between his knees and takes aim. He flips the ball underhand toward the basket.

The player is not goofing off. No one is snickering about a "sissy" style of free-throw shooting. That's because the shooter happens to be one of the best free-throw shooters in pro basketball history. Using the old-fashioned, underhand method, Rick Barry led the league in free-throw percentage nine times. In 1978–79 he made an incredible 94.7 percent of his foul shots!

As the last of the underhand free-throw shooters, Barry obviously cared nothing about peer pressure. His disdain for other people's opinions launched him on one of the stormiest basketball careers of his time. He started out feuding with his coach as an All-State star at Roselle Park High School in New Jersey. In the late 1960s and early 1970s, he irritated almost everyone by jumping back and forth from one league to another. Barry was the first big star to abandon the NBA and sign with the new American Basketball Association (ABA) in 1967. After a court action required him to sit out a year, Barry played for the Oakland Oaks. Then in 1972, after more lawsuits, he ended up back with Golden State of the NBA.

Fortunately for Barry, he found smooth sailing at the time when he really needed it. His University of Miami coach, Bruce Hale, "made me a pro in college," according to Barry.[1] Hale often put three defenders at a time on Barry in practice to toughen him up for his future pro career. Barry responded by leading the nation's college scorers in 1964–65 with an average of 37.4 points a game. Although thinner than most opponents, he outscrapped them for 18 rebounds per game.

As the No. 1 draft choice of the San Francisco Warriors, Barry poured in 25.7 points a game in 1965–66. His 2,059 points broke the rookie record for NBA forwards. The following year, he established himself as a top star. First, he scored 38 points to win Most Valuable Player honors in the All-Star Game. Then, he ended Wilt Chamberlain's seven-year stranglehold on the NBA scoring title, scoring 35.6 points per game. Finally, he led the Warriors to the NBA Finals against the Philadelphia 76ers, where he averaged 40 points in a losing effort.

After bouncing around from league to league, he returned to the Warriors for his finest year as a pro. In 1974–75, he led the underdog Warriors into the Finals against the Washington Bullets. Barry took pride in proving that he was more than just a scorer. "If I'm not shooting well, I'll try to be an asset in other ways—like defense, passing, rebounding and hustle," he said.[2] With Barry playing his finest all-around game, the Warriors shocked the Bullets in four straight games to claim the title. Barry was named NBA Finals MVP.

RICK BARRY

BORN: March 28, 1944, Elizabeth, New Jersey.

HIGH SCHOOL: Roselle Park High School, Roselle Park, New Jersey.

COLLEGE: University of Miami, Florida.

PRO: San Francisco Warriors, 1965–1967; Oakland Oaks (ABA), 1968–1969; Washington Capitols (ABA), 1969–1970; New York Nets (ABA), 1970–1972; Golden State Warriors, 1972–1978; Houston Rockets, 1978–1980.

RECORDS: Shares single-game record for most free throws made in one quarter, 14; Shares NBA Finals single-game record for most field goals made, 22.

HONORS: NBA free-throw percentage leader, 1969, 1971–1973, 1975–1976, 1978–1980; NBA All-Star, 1966–1967, 1973–1978; NBA Rookie of the Year, 1966; NBA scoring leader, 1967; NBA All-Star MVP, 1967; NBA Finals MVP, 1975; elected to Basketball Hall of Fame, 1987.

Having gotten by the defense, Rick Barry lays the ball in for two points.

Internet Address

http://www.nba.com/history/barry_bio.html

ELGIN BAYLOR

Driving to the basket, Elgin Baylor tries to squeeze past the Boston defender.

FEW PEOPLE WOULD CHOOSE A JOB in a furniture store over the chance at a pro basketball career. Elgin Baylor did. Pro basketball was neither popular nor high-paying when he was growing up in Washington, D.C. Because African Americans were not allowed on public playgrounds, he never played the game until he was fourteen. Even though he immediately made All-City as a freshman, Baylor had no use for school or for basketball. He dropped out to work at the furniture store.

Fortunately, his mother persuaded him to return to school. Baylor went on to become the first African American selected as a high school All-American. Because of basketball, Baylor ended up where he never dreamed he would be—in college. Scoring more than 31 points and grabbing a college-record 23.5 rebounds per game, Baylor led Seattle University to second place in the 1958 NCAA tournament.

In pro basketball, Baylor continued to be ahead of his time. In an era of dominating giant centers and expert shooters, Baylor played a different brand of basketball. Although only six-feet five-inches, he could score from in close with his explosive quickness and power. He was the first to fake out opponents while hanging in midair, and bank shots off the glass from impossible angles. Had he played later, when basketball grew more popular, his highlight-film heroics would have rivaled those of Michael Jordan and Julius Erving.

At whatever level he played, Baylor immediately became a star. He finished fourth in the NBA in scoring (24.9 points per game) and third in rebounding (15.8) during his rookie season with the Minneapolis Lakers. In 1960–61, he was unstoppable. His combination of 34.8 points and 19.8 rebounds per game will probably never be equaled by any other forward.

Shortly after the Lakers moved to Los Angeles, guard Jerry West joined the Lakers. Baylor and West formed a one-two punch that put the Lakers near the top of the standings every year.

Unfortunately, Baylor played in the shadow of a great player and a great team.

The year after Baylor entered the NBA, Wilt Chamberlain arrived. Had Chamberlain not come along, Baylor would have been the greatest scorer in league history. But despite Baylor's astounding numbers, he could never beat out Chamberlain for the scoring title. Baylor scored an astounding 71 points in one game in 1960, then Chamberlain topped it by tallying 100 in a single game in 1962.

Even more frustrating was Baylor's quest for an NBA championship. Year after year his Lakers reached the finals but could never get past the great Boston Celtics teams. Baylor made heroic efforts to top the Celtics. In Game 5 of the 1962 championship, he dominated the Celtics' best defender, Satch Sanders. After Baylor collected 61 points and 22 rebounds, Sanders could only shake his head and say, "Elgin was just a machine."[1] Even in agonizing defeat, Baylor showed he was something special.

ELGIN BAYLOR

BORN: September 16, 1934, Washington, District of Columbia.

HIGH SCHOOL: Phelps Vocational High School; Springarn High School, Washington, District of Columbia.

COLLEGE: College of Idaho; Seattle University.

PRO: Minneapolis Lakers, 1958–1960; Los Angeles Lakers, 1960–1972.

RECORDS: Holds NBA Finals single-game record for most points scored in a game, 61; holds All-Star Game career record for most free throws made, 78.

HONORS: NBA Rookie of the Year, 1959; NBA All-Star Co-MVP, 1960; NBA All-Star, 1959–1965, 1967–1970; elected to Basketball Hall of Fame, 1976.

Baylor is one of the greatest playoff performers of all-time. He had career averages of 27 points and 12.9 rebounds per game in the postseason.

Internet Address

http://www.nba.com/history/baylor_bio.html

LARRY BIRD

Larry Bird shoots over the outstretched arms of Magic Johnson.

LARRY BIRD

JUST BEFORE THE NBA THREE-POINT shooting contest at the 1986 All-Star Game, Larry Bird walked into the locker room. Looking around at his opponents in the contest he announced, "All right, which of you is going to finish second?"[1] Even though some teased him as "the hick from French Lick" because of his rural upbringing, confidence on the court was never a problem for Bird. After issuing his challenge, he backed it up by winning the shooting contest.

Bird's fierce competitiveness came from battling his older brothers at their home in the small town of French Lick, Indiana. His first love was baseball. But when one of his brothers became the town hero by winning a high school basketball game, Larry took that as a challenge. Anything a brother could do, Larry could do better. Soon Larry would become the town hero.

During his entire thirteen-year career, Bird never led the NBA in any category except for his four free-throw shooting titles. He could not jump well or run fast. Yet, playing against such top opponents as Magic Johnson and Michael Jordan, Bird walked off with three straight NBA Most Valuable Player Awards in the 1980s.

Bird did not need to outsprint and outleap opponents. Constant hours of practice made him one of the league's deadliest shots. He also ranked as one of the league's best rebounders and smartest passers. With his quick hands, he recorded more than 1,500 steals. Bird became only the fifth NBA player to score 20,000 points, grab 5,000 rebounds, and notch 5,000 assists.

What made Bird great was his steel nerves under

pressure. "In the closing seconds of every game, I want the ball in my hands for that last shot—not in anybody else's," he said.[2] More often than not, Bird came through.

But although he thrived on competitive pressure, he had trouble handling the stress of fast-paced city life. Even after a career of performing before millions of fans, he said, "I don't like crowds. Never have."[3] His dislike of crowds nearly destroyed his chance at a pro career. Following high school, he lasted only a few months at Indiana University before dropping out. He was not comfortable being at a school that was so large.

Fortunately, Bird found a smaller, lesser-known college where he could grow into a star. At Indiana State University, Bird often drove his team to victory through sheer willpower. He took a mediocre team all the way to the NCAA Championship Game in 1979 before losing to Magic Johnson's Michigan State Spartans.

Bird worked the same magic on the Boston Celtics. Boston had lost 52 games the year before Bird arrived. He immediately turned things around, leading the Celtics to a 61–21 mark. In the process, he got some revenge by beating out Johnson for Rookie of the Year award.

At six-feet nine-inches, Bird is the largest of the small forwards in this book. He started out as a power forward. But with the arrival of six-foot eleven-inch Kevin McHale in 1980, Bird switched to small forward, to anchor one of the top front lines in NBA history.

LARRY BIRD

BORN: December 7, 1956, West Baden, Indiana.

HIGH SCHOOL: Springs Valley High School, French Lick, Indiana.

COLLEGE: Indiana University; Indiana State University.

PRO: Boston Celtics, 1979–1992.

RECORDS: Holds NBA career playoff record for most defensive rebounds, 1,323.

HONORS: NBA Rookie of the Year, 1980; NBA All-Star, 1980–1992; NBA MVP, 1984–1986; NBA Finals MVP, 1984, 1986; NBA All-Star MVP, 1982; NBA free-throw percentage leader, 1984, 1986–1987, 1990; NBA Coach of the Year, 1998; elected to Basketball Hall of Fame, 1998.

Dribbling into the paint, Larry Bird looks to make a play.

Internet Address

http://www.nba.com/history/bird_bio.html

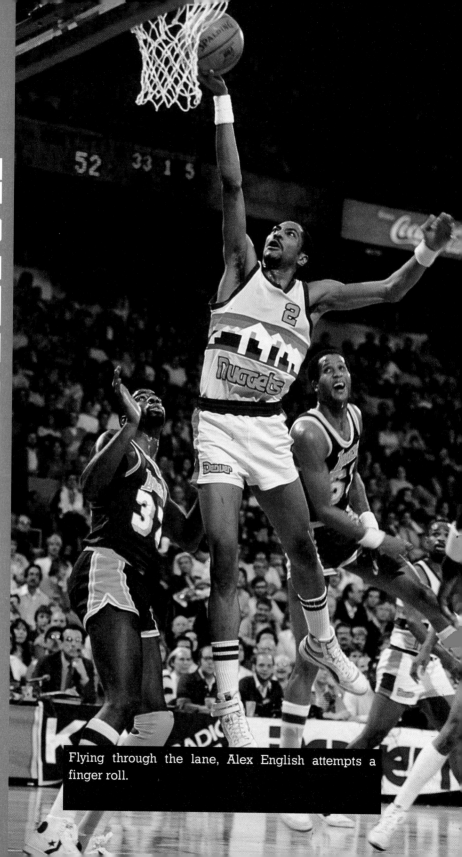

ALEX ENGLISH

Flying through the lane, Alex English attempts a finger roll.

ALEX ENGLISH MAY BE THE QUIETEST scorer who ever played in the NBA. Hardly anyone noticed that he won the league scoring title or that he ranked near the top of the league in scoring for eight straight years.

Maybe it was because no one expected English to amount to much. Although he started every game of his four-year career at the University of South Carolina, he did not impress the pros. They did not believe the rail-thin six-foot seven-inch forward could stand up to the pounding of muscular NBA forwards. The Milwaukee Bucks waited until the second round of the 1976 draft to select him. Then, after English spent two uneventful seasons as a benchwarmer, they cut him.

The Indiana Pacers signed him in 1978. English responded with 16 points and 8 rebounds per game. Yet the Pacers traded him away in 1979. English moved on to Denver, where he boosted his scoring average to nearly 24 points per game. Even then he could not get respect. Denver tried to trade him to the San Diego Clippers. To add insult to injury, the Clippers turned down the offer. As Denver Nuggets coach Doug Moe remarked about the deal, "Thank God, there are people in this world dumber than me."[1]

English did most of his scoring in the bruising no-man's-land near the basket. Normally, only the very tall, powerful, or quick players could consistently score from in close. English was shorter and thinner than virtually all his opponents, and not exceptionally quick. He did not appear to be particularly graceful or athletic when he flipped his awkward running shots through the net. "I guess that my game has kind of an off-balance flow," English explained.[2]

When he went up for a shot, it looked as if his opponents were certain to block it. Somehow, though, English knew exactly when to pull the trigger, and he could get his arms fully extended so that taller players could not reach his shot. He finished his career with a shooting percentage of better than 50 percent.

Perhaps English escaped notice because of his personality. Unlike many of his flashy opponents, who enjoyed being the center of attention, English was quiet and thoughtful. He had made himself into an accomplished creative writer who published a couple of volumes of poetry. English took more interest in social causes than in winning product endorsements. One year he persuaded his fellow players to donate their pay from the All-Star Game to help the hungry in Ethiopia.

Whatever the reason, no player has accomplished more while being noticed so little. In 1983, he won the scoring title with a 28.4 point average. From 1982 to 1989, he played in eight straight All-Star games. At the time of his retirement, he had scored more career baskets than all but three stars who ever played the game. There is no doubt that Alex English quietly made his mark on the NBA.

ALEX ENGLISH

BORN: January 5, 1954, Columbia, South Carolina.

HIGH SCHOOL: Dreher High School, Columbia, South Carolina.

COLLEGE: University of South Carolina.

PRO: Milwaukee Bucks, 1976–1978; Indiana Pacers, 1978–1979; Denver Nuggets, 1979–1990; Dallas Mavericks, 1990–1991.

HONORS: NBA All-Star, 1982–1989; NBA scoring leader, 1983; elected to Basketball Hall of Fame, 1997.

After his basketball career ended, English finally got the credit he deserved. He was inducted into the Naismith Memorial Basketball Hall of Fame in 1997.

Internet Address

http://www.nba.com/history/english_bio.html

JULIUS ERVING

Larry Bird (number thirty-three) can only watch as Julius Erving pulls up for an uncontested jumper.

THE GAME OF BASKETBALL CHANGED the moment Julius Erving first launched himself into the air from the free-throw line. He soared into space, holding the ball high in his huge hands. As the fans gasped, "the Doctor" sailed to the basket and slammed the ball through the net. On playgrounds across the country, young athletes started experimenting with their own creative, rim-rattling slams. Erving had lit the fuse on an explosion that turned the NBA from a struggling league into the hottest sports show on the planet.

Everyone called him "Doctor J," thinking it was a tribute to his basketball skill. Actually, the name was a joke from Erving's childhood on Long Island in New York. "A friend of mine kept telling me he was going to be a professor, so I told him I was going to be a doctor, and we started calling each other that," says Erving.[1]

When he was three, Erving was abandoned by his father. He spent much of his time alone on the streets. There he learned the game of basketball, which he saw as his ticket to success.

More than a hundred colleges recruited him out of high school. He chose the University of Massachusetts, where spectators came to games early to watch him warm up. After averaging 26.9 points and leading the nation in rebounding in 1971 as a junior, Erving left school to turn pro. He signed with the Virginia Squires of the ABA. In his second season, Erving won the ABA scoring title with a 31.9 average.

The Squires ran short of money and traded Erving to the

New York Nets. Even in New York, the ABA attracted few fans, and as a result few saw the Doctor operating at his best. No one had ever seen such acrobatic moves to the basket. "Sometimes when I start a play," he said, "I never know if I will be able to do what I would like. But I always go ahead and try. I have confidence in my ability as a basketball player."[2]

Following the 1976 season, four of the ABA teams were accepted into the NBA in a merger. Erving, now traded to the Philadelphia 76ers, had some trouble adjusting to the new league. Boston coach Red Auerbach scoffed, "The ABA was a minor league; over here, Erving is just another small forward."[3] But in that year's All-Star Game, the Doctor toyed with the NBA's greatest players. He scored 30 points and grabbed 12 rebounds to win the game's Most Valuable Player award.

Erving made the All-Star team every year he played. In 1983, he capped his career by sinking a jump shot to seal the 76ers' championship win over the Lakers. Including his ABA career, the Doctor became only the third pro player to score thirty thousand points.

Not only did he display great talent and flair, he was a class act. "I've never heard anybody knock him or express jealousy," said former Atlanta forward Dominique Wilkins. "I can't name you one other player who has that status."[4]

JULIUS ERVING

BORN: February 22, 1950, Long Island, New York.

HIGH SCHOOL: Roosevelt High School, Long Island, New York.

COLLEGE: University of Massachusetts.

PRO: Virginia Squires (ABA), 1971–1973; New York Nets (ABA), 1973–1976; Philadelphia 76ers, 1976–1987.

RECORDS: (ABA) Highest career scoring average, 28.7 ppg.

HONORS: ABA MVP, 1974–1976; ABA All-Star, 1972–1974; NBA All-Star, 1977–1987; NBA MVP, 1981; NBA All-Star MVP, 1977, 1983; elected to Basketball Hall of Fame, 1993.

Rising high above the basket, Julius Erving throws down a slam dunk.

Internet Address

http://www.nba.com/history/erving_bio.html

JOHN HAVLICEK

With his eyes on the basket, John Havlicek of the Boston Celtics elevates for the field-goal attempt.

JOHN HAVLICEK

FIVE SECONDS LEFT. It is Game 7 of the 1965 playoff series between the champion Boston Celtics and the talented Philadelphia 76ers. Boston leads by one point, but Philadelphia has the ball. As the 76ers put the ball in play, Boston's John Havlicek is guarding Chet Walker. Out of the corner of his eye, he sees the pass being thrown. With the reflexes of a cobra, Havlicek darts in front of Walker and steals the pass. Game over. Boston goes on to win yet another NBA title.

Many Boston Celtics fans consider that the greatest play in the team's proud history. It launched third-year reserve forward John Havlicek on his way to becoming an NBA legend.

Few believed the six-foot five-inch Havlicek would be more than a role player when he entered the league in 1963. He had been a defensive specialist on the 1960 NCAA champion Ohio State Buckeyes in college. Boston's Hall of Fame guard Bob Cousy decided the rookie was a "non-shooter who would probably burn himself out."[1]

But Havlicek had learned something while concentrating on defense in college. "I realized then that the most difficult player to guard is the kind of player who is always moving."[2]

Havlicek's stamina amazed his teammates. "You just wind him up and—click, click, click—he keeps going," said All-Pro center Bill Russell.[3]

From the first practice, Boston coach Red Auerbach knew he'd stumbled upon a special player. The problem was where to play him. Hondo, as everyone called

Havlicek, was small for an NBA forward. Auerbach at first tried to turn him into a guard. But by Hondo's third year in the league, the coach had found a way to make use of his unique skills—as a reserve small forward. Havlicek came off the bench to spark his team and to disrupt the opponents. He was so good at it that he was named captain of his team, an honor he held for more than a decade.

Havlicek was a hopeless perfectionist. From running precise offensive plays to always hanging his sweat socks on a hanger, Havlicek insisted on doing things in a certain exact way. His attention to detail made him one of the best two-way players in NBA history. Beginning in 1968, Havlicek was a fixture on the league's All-Defensive team. At the same time, he led Boston in scoring ten times and in assists six times. In one season, 1969–70, he led the team in rebounding as well as in scoring and assists, and remained the team's top defender. Havlicek was a main reason that the Celtics won eight NBA titles during his career, often against teams with more talent.

But Havlicek's proudest moment came on November 20, 1977. It was his 1,123rd pro game, more than anyone else had ever played. "If there's any phase of basketball I've been identified with, it's endurance," he said. "When I broke the old record, it meant a great deal to me."[4]

JOHN HAVLICEK

BORN: April 8, 1940, Martins Ferry, Ohio.

HIGH SCHOOL: Bridgeport High School, Bridgeport, Ohio.

COLLEGE: Ohio State University.

PRO: Boston Celtics, 1962–1978.

RECORDS: Shares NBA Finals single-game record for most points in an overtime period, 9.

HONORS: NBA leader in minutes played, 1971, 1976; NBA All-Star, 1966–1978; NBA Finals MVP, 1974; elected to Basketball Hall of Fame, 1983.

Havlicek was a member of eight NBA championship teams with the Boston Celtics. He won the 1974 NBA Finals MVP Award.

Internet Address

http://www.nba.com/history/havlicek_bio.html

GRANT HILL

"ONE OF THE FIRST THINGS I remember is being conscious of trying to fit in," says Grant Hill.[1] That has not been easy. Fame has stuck to Grant Hill like a tattoo ever since he was born. As the only child of the Dallas Cowboys' star running back Calvin Hill, Grant received far more attention than he wanted. When his dad came to Grant's junior high to speak to students, Grant hid in the nurses' office, pretending to be sick.

Family fame prevented Grant Hill from playing his favorite game—football. Fearing injury and not wanting Grant to be saddled with living up to his dad's reputation, Calvin Hill refused to allow his son to play the game. Grant settled for basketball.

Playing at Duke University, Hill enjoyed a few years of being relatively unknown. "In college I was just known as Grant Hill, the tall guy who lives down the hall," he remembers.[2] That was because Duke focused on team play rather than featuring stars. While Hill never averaged as much as 20 points a game during his four years at Duke, his steady team play helped the Blue Devils to win national titles in 1991 and 1992.

But fame was lurking around the corner, waiting to grab him. Hill joined the woeful Detroit Pistons as their No. 1 draft choice in 1993. Suddenly, Hill burst into the spotlight. Here was a man who stood six-feet eight-inches, who could score, pass, dribble, rebound, block shots, and play defense. Teammate Joe Dumars declared, "He's the best player I've seen coming into the league in ten years."[3]

Hill arrived at a time when fans were growing irritated

GRANT HILL

Putting the ball on the floor, Grant Hill makes a move past his defender.

with the rude behavior of many of the game's younger stars. Hill was a genuinely nice person with respect for the game and for others. "I've never derived pleasure from making someone else feel bad or angry," he explained.[4]

Hill's all-around athletic play and positive attitude were like a breath of fresh air. Only a few weeks into his rookie season, he suddenly became a favorite of fans everywhere. He became the first rookie to receive the most votes in balloting for the All-Star Game. Hill did not let it go to his head. "I think all things need improvement in my game," he said.[5] He wasn't even sure he belonged on the All-Star team.

That changed when he played on the United States Olympic team in 1996 with many of the top NBA stars. "If I began in awe of those guys, I didn't end up that way."[6] After practicing with the NBA's best, Hill realized that he had more skill and maturity than most of his rivals.

Now he's out to prove that he is the man who can bring a title to Detroit. Unfortunately, his play has made people talk of him as the next Michael Jordan. First Calvin Hill's son, now Michael Jordan's successor—Grant Hill just cannot shake those comparisons.

GRANT HILL

BORN: October 5, 1972, Dallas, Texas.

HIGH SCHOOL: South Lakes High School, Reston, Virginia.

COLLEGE: Duke University.

PRO: Detroit Pistons, 1994– .

HONORS: NBA Co-Rookie of the Year, 1994; NBA All-Star,
1994–1998.

Grant Hill is considered to be one of the best all-around players in
the NBA. Opposing teams have to prepare for his passing ability,
as well as his scoring and rebounding.

Internet Address

http://www.nba.com/playerfile/grant_hill.html

SCOTTIE PIPPEN

Moving with the ball, Scottie Pippen looks to make a pass.

SCOTTIE PIPPEN HAS LIVED his pro career under a giant shadow. According to former NBA great Bill Walton, "You think about it, Scottie Pippen might just be the second-best all-around player in the league."[1] Yet most people have not paid much attention to Pippen because he played on the same team as the best basketball player on the planet— Michael Jordan.

Even Michael Jordan, however, could not win basketball titles by himself. Jordan never succeeded until Pippen came along. According to Chicago Bulls coach Phil Jackson, "The reason we were able to win championships was the development of Scottie Pippen."[2]

That development came slowly. Pippen did not win a starting position until his senior year of high school. Colleges were not interested in him. Pippen's high school coach had to persuade an old friend at a small college to take Pippen on as the team's *manager*! While at the University of Central Arkansas, though, Pippen grew from just over six-feet to six-feet seven-inches. He lost none of his coordination during that growth spurt, and he won a spot on the team.

After Pippen averaged over 23 points per game in his senior season, the Seattle SuperSonics drafted him in the first round. Almost immediately, the Bulls made a draft-day trade to obtain Pippen's services. It was a gamble. "I never heard of him or his school," said Jordan.[3]

Jordan demanded a lot from himself and from his teammates. Pippen had to learn to deal with pressure and criticism. In Game 6 of a tight 1989 playoff series against the champion Detroit Pistons, Pippen was knocked out by an elbow to the head. He could not return to the game. The Bulls lost the game and the series.

The following year, Pippen got a migraine headache just before the seventh and deciding game of the playoff series against Detroit. The pain was so terrible he could not play. Again, the Bulls lost, and fans questioned Pippen's courage.

They also questioned his attitude after the 1994 Eastern Conference Finals. Playing without Jordan that year, the Bulls were battling New York in a tight game with 1.8 seconds left. Coach Jackson called for Toni Kukoc to take the final shot. Upset that he was not chosen for the honor, Pippen refused to go back on the court.

Looking back on these incidents, Pippen says, "I wanted everything to happen in a certain way; when it didn't, I didn't handle it."[4] But he learned from every hardship. He changed his diet, got more sleep, and began listening to advice from older players. He welcomed the challenge of guarding Michael Jordan every day in practice.

With his spidery arms and quick feet, Pippen became the top defensive forward in the game. Pippen and Jordan formed an unstoppable combination that rolled to six NBA titles. After the 1997–98 season, Jordan retired. Pippen was traded to the Houston Rockets. Now he would try to win another title, this time alongside Charles Barkley and Hakeem Olajuwon.

How did Pippen make the jump from team manager to a future Hall of Fame forward? Even Pippen is baffled by his success. "The answer is, I don't know," he says. "I guess it just happens."[5]

Scottie Pippen

Born: September 25, 1965, Hamburg, Arkansas.

High School: Hamburg High School, Hamburg, Arkansas.

College: University of Central Arkansas.

Pro: Chicago Bulls, 1987–98; Houston Rockets, 1999– .

Records: Shares NBA Finals single-game record for most three-point field goals made in one game, 7.

Honors: NBA All-Star, 1990, 1992–1998; NBA All-Star MVP, 1994.

Since coming into the league, Pippen has been part of eight championship teams. He won six with the Chicago Bulls and was a member of gold-medal-winning Olympic teams in 1992 and 1996.

Internet Address

http://www.nba.com/playerfile/scottie_pippen.html

GLEN RICE

Glen Rice is one of the most prolific scorers in basketball. He finished in the top ten in the league in scoring average in both 1996–97 and 1997–98.

GLEN RICE KNOWS HOW TO IMPRESS the right people. The greatest basketball players in history were gathered for a special celebration at the 1997 All-Star Game when Rice entered the action. These Hall of Famers witnessed the greatest shooting exhibition in All-Star history. Rice pumped in four three-point shots within two minutes. He ended up with a record 20 points in the third quarter alone and won the game's Most Valuable Player honors in a landslide.

Rice has built his reputation as a sharpshooter. Long-range shooters usually have hot and cold streaks. But as Rice's college teammate, Terry Mills, noted in Rice's break-through season of 1996–97, "Streaks last a week. Glen's been tearing up the league for more than a month now."[1]

Rice agreed. "I've been in zones before when you feel like anything you put up is going in. This feels different. It feels like this is the way it's going to be."[2]

Rice credits practice and small hands as the keys to his success. He does not have perfect form when he shoots. But he has practiced his own style faithfully since he was a small boy, shooting baskets in the dark. "Funny, they used to talk about my little brother Kevin's shot. They said he had perfect form and that my shot was sloppy. But mine went in and his didn't."[3]

Coaches marvel at his quick release, especially on three-point shots. As soon as he catches the ball, it's on its way toward the net. "Most guys need a lot of leg and extra oomph from that far out," says Coach Kevin Loughery, "But

Glen uses very little energy on his shot, just a flick of the wrist."[4]

That marvelously smooth shot first hit the national scene in 1989. That year Rice set a new NCAA tournament record by scoring 184 points in six games for the University of Michigan. His 31 points and 11 rebounds led Michigan to victory in the championship game.

The Miami Heat made him the fourth overall selection in the 1989 draft. Working mainly from long range, Rice averaged nearly 20 points per game for the Heat over six seasons. On November 2, 1995, he was crushed when he learned he had been traded to the Charlotte Hornets. But he recovered after meeting Cristina Fernandez. So intent was Rice on impressing his new girlfriend that he poured in 56 points the day of their first date.

By the middle of the next season, Rice turned himself into a topflight NBA superstar. He improved his scoring average to 26.8 points per game by driving to the basket and drawing fouls.

But the jump shot remained his trademark. In 1996–97, Rice led the league with 207 three-point baskets. He made an astounding 47 percent of his long-range tries. For Rice, however, the only surprise was that he ever missed. As Assistant Coach T. R. Dunn commented, "The only thing more consistent than Glen's jumper is his confidence in his jumper."[5]

During the 1999 season, Rice was traded to the Los Angeles Lakers in exchange for Eddie Jones and Elden Campbell. The trade added a deadly jump-shooter to a Lakers team that already included all-stars Kobe Bryant and Shaquille O'Neal.

GLEN RICE

BORN: May 28, 1967, Flint, Michigan.

HIGH SCHOOL: Northwestern Community High School, Flint, Michigan.

COLLEGE: University of Michigan.

PRO: Miami Heat, 1989–1995; Charlotte Hornets, 1995–1999. Los Angeles Lakers, 1999– .

RECORDS: Holds All-Star Game record for most points in one half, 24.

HONORS: NBA All-Star MVP, 1997; NBA All-Star, 1996–1998; NBA three-point percentage leader, 1997.

Gliding through the air, Glen Rice releases a shot before Greg Ostertag can provide the defense.

Internet Address

http://www.nba.com/playerfile/glen_rice.html

CHAPTER NOTES

Introduction

1. Generally attributed to George Leybourne's poem "The Man on the Flying Trapeze," first published in 1860.

Paul Arizin

1. "Basketball Champ," *Newsweek*, March 17, 1952, p. 62.
2. *Great Athletes: The Twentieth Century*, vol. 1 (Pasadena, Calif.: Salem Press, 1992), p. 76.

Rick Barry

1. *Great Athletes: The Twentieth Century*, vol. 2 (Pasadena, Calif.: Salem Press, 1992), p. 145.
2. Howard E. Ferguson, *The Edge: The Guide to Fulfilling Dreams, Maximizing Success and Enjoying a Lifetime of Achievement* (Cleveland, Ohio: Getting the Edge Company, 1990), p. 5:34.

Elgin Baylor

1. Edward Dolan, *The NBA's Greatest Moments* (New York: Watts, 1982), p. 47.

Larry Bird

1. "Dateline," *Sports Illustrated*, February 17, 1997, p. 26.
2. Howard E. Ferguson, *The Edge: The Guide to Fulfilling Dreams, Maximizing Success and Enjoying a Lifetime of Achievement* (Cleveland, Ohio: Getting the Edge Company, 1990), p. 6:7.
3. Jackie McMullen, "Back Home Again in Indiana," *Sports Illustrated*, October 27, 1997, p. 102.

Alex English

1. Jack McCallum, "English Is Spoken Here," *Sports Illustrated*, December 9, 1985, p. 58.
2. Ibid., p. 57.

Julius Erving

1. Gene Brown, ed., *The New York Times' Encyclopedia of Sports*, vol. 3. (New York: The New York Times, 1969), p. 178.
2. Howard E. Ferguson, *The Edge: The Guide to Fulfilling Dreams, Maximizing Success and Enjoying a Lifetime of Achievement* (Cleveland, Ohio: Getting the Edge Company, 1990), p. 4:17.
3. Curry Kirkpatrick, "The Master of Midair," *Sports Illustrated*, May 4, 1987, p. 81.

4. Jack McCallum, "Doc Across America," *Sports Illustrated*, May 4, 1987, p. 74.

John Havlicek

1. "It's the End of a Long Run," *Sports Illustrated*, April 10, 1978, p. 28.
2. Herbert Warren Wind, "The Complete Basketball Player," *New Yorker*, March 28, 1977, p. 88.
3. Ibid.
4. Ibid., p. 87.

Grant Hill

1. Jack McCallum, "The Man," *Sports Illustrated*, November 25, 1996, p. 47.
2. Tom Singer, "Grant Hill: One on One," *Sport*, April 1996, pp. 18–19.
3. *Street & Smith's Pro Basketball 96–97* (New York: Ballantine Books, 1996), p. 33.
4. Ibid.
5. *Street & Smith's Pro Basketball 95–96* (New York: Ballantine Books, 1995), p. 51.
6. McCallum, p. 42.

Scottie Pippen

1. Leigh Montville, "Out of the Shadow," *Sports Illustrated*, February 24, 1992, p. 77.
2. *Street & Smith's Pro Basketball 93–94* (New York: Ballantine Books, 1993), p. 20.
3. Ibid.
4. *Street & Smith's Pro Basketball 96–97* (New York: Ballantine Books, 1996), p. 39.
5. Montville, p. 84.

Glen Rice

1. Phil Taylor, "To the Hoop, Hon," *Sports Illustrated*, February 24, 1997, p. 34.
2. Ibid., p. 35.
3. *Street & Smith's Pro Basketball 92–93* (New York: Ballantine Books, 1992), p. 32.
4. Ibid.
5. Taylor, p. 34.

INDEX

DATE DUE

OCT 0 4			
OCT 3 1			
JAN 2 9			
MAY 1 0			
JUN 0			
APR 1 5 2002			
MAY 0 8 2002			
NOV 2 1			
FEB 0 3			
FEB 2 1			
MAR 1 7			
FEB 0 7			
FEB 1 4			
JUN 0 3			
FEB 2 4			
MAR 2 8			
MAY 3 0			